THE GREAT MASTERS OF DRAWING

DRAWINGS BY

BOTTICELLI

BY

ALDO BERTINI

TRANSLATED BY

FLORENCE H. PHILLIPS

DOVER PUBLICATIONS, INC., NEW YORK

Published in Canada by
GENERAL PUBLISHING COMPANY, LTD.,
30 LESMILL ROAD, DON MILLS, TORONTO, ONTARIO.

Botticelli is a new translation, first published by Dover Publications, Inc., in 1968, of the work first published by Aldo Martello, Milan, 1953, in his series "I Grandi Maestri del Disegno." The present edition, which contains all the original illustrations, is published by special arrangement with Mr. Martello.

Library of Congress Catalog Card Number: 67-27876

Manufactured in the United States of America

DOVER PUBLICATIONS, INC.
180 VARICK STREET, NEW YORK, N.Y. 10014

BOTTICELLI'S DRAWINGS

THERE is perhaps no artist whose work brings the word "dream" so spontaneously and appropriately to mind as Botticelli in his paintings: "dream" in its sense of pure contemplation or poetry, escape from reality permeated by a pungent vein of melancholy. In each of the various periods of his life Botticelli's works evoked this feeling—from the *Primavera*, to *The Birth of Venus*, to the London *Nativity*—and it is this quality which was rediscovered with new understanding and awareness by nineteenth-century art historians. They recognized that Botticelli was one of those great and original artists who have truly created a new absolute standard of beauty.

This, however, is not the place for an abstract discussion of Botticelli's transparent, enchanted world. Whether this world took the form of a bloody episode from the Bible or Roman history, a pagan or Christian myth, or even a portrait, it was always an incarnation of anguished beauty, which in the final period of the artist's life became so passionate that his works from that time seem almost convulsive. But even genius cannot exist outside history, and the contribution of the contemporary art historians who have succeeded the Romantics of the last century has been to set Botticelli's style within a precise historical framework.

He began very strictly in the manner of Fra Lippo Lippi, as is evidenced by his great painting in London, *The Adoration of the Magi*, which actually used to be attributed to Filippo Lippi. Subsequently, however, he went on to assimilate in an entirely original manner the sense of form which characterized the works of Pollaiuolo and Verrocchio, and the quality of expressive emphasis which was to be found in the paintings of Andrea del Castagno. From this period the outstanding masterpieces are the *Judith* and the *Portrait of an Unknown Man with a Medal* in the Uffizi, the *St. Sebastian* in the Berlin Staatliche Museen and the *Madonna of the Eucharist* in the Gardner Museum in Boston. People who justly recognize contour line to be the most characteristic formal element of Botticelli's paintings have tended to exaggerate his relationship to Pollaiuolo, the artist who most consistently used this expressive technique. The unique quality of Botticelli's line, already clearly distinguishable in his youthful paintings, is often just as energetic as Pollaiuolo's line. Pollaiuolo aimed at a more centralized and monumental representation based especially on an effect of spatial perspective; hence his predilection for foreshortening, avoided by the younger master. Botticelli's paintings are predominantly composed from a frontal viewpoint, parallel to the front plane, through which his line runs either sinuously or angularly; these characteristics are what led Berenson and Lionello Venturi to speak of his "presentation" rather than his "representation."

Botticelli's exquisite plastic sense, which he used to explore psychological nuance, does, on the other hand, relate strongly to Verrocchio. It is also reminiscent of Leonardo, as is the subtlety of certain inflections of his line, but Botticelli did not at all share Leonardo's concern for chiaroscuro as the essential element of painting. His color, as has so often been observed, in no way distracts the eye from the play of plastic and linear elements in his paintings, but he did use it strikingly for special accents, and toward the end of his life, as Lionello Venturi has trenchantly pointed out, he began to experiment in a particularly original manner with the use of color for contrasts. Thus it is not such a tiresomely obvious statement to say that the draughtsmanship of Botticelli is clearly evident in his paintings; on the other hand, his drawings (in the strict sense) reveal the originality of his vision in an even more fundamental and spare way than do the paintings, and this is what gives them their extraordinary importance. Even Vasari, who was not overly enthusiastic in his opinions of Botticelli's art, wrote of the drawings: "Sandro drew unusually well; so much so that for some time after him artists did their best to obtain his drawings, and we ourselves have several in our book which were executed with great skill and judgment."

Unfortunately only a meagre number of the drawings have survived, with the exception of the series illustrating *The Divine Comedy*. They are so scarce, in fact, that in the present volume I have included several drawings from the school of Botticelli which seem to me to exemplify certain of the master's concepts. On the other hand, I have unhesitatingly omitted the drawing of *St. Jerome* in the Uffizi, because despite its unanimous attribution to Botticelli, its quality is so inferior. The exclusion of certain other drawings, such as the *Drapery for the lower part of a figure* (Uffizi), the *Small head of an angel in a circle* (British Museum) and the *Miracle of St. John the Evangelist* (Louvre), is due purely to circumstances. I hope that eventually new discoveries and attributions will result from a complete reappraisal of all the material known, and that certain drawings now attributed to Filippino Lippi will undergo particular scrutiny. For the moment, however, youthful drawings by Botticelli are extraordinarily rare, and thus it is tempting to concur in Ragghianti's astute suggestion that the Rennes *Head of an angel* (Plate 1), formerly attributed to Piero del Pollaiuolo, be considered a Botticelli, as this would provide us with our only drawing from his "Pollaiuolo-Verrocchio period," the period of the *Fortitude*. The Rennes drawing seems particularly close to Verrocchio, both in technique and in form, as shown by a comparison with the famous *Head of an angel* (Uffizi 130 E) assumed to be a study for *The Baptism of Christ*. (The latter drawing has also been attributed to Leonardo, but it is certainly by Verrocchio.) In any case, despite the impossibility of viewing the Rennes drawing in relation to other undisputed drawings from the same period, the hypothetical attribution of it to Botticelli, based on a comparison with his paintings, is confirmed by the later development of his style.

His earliest known drawing of unquestionable attribution is the *Three angels in a lunette* (page 1). This exceptionally beautiful study is indeed stylistically related to Verrocchio and Leonardo, though it belongs to the same (later) period as the *Primavera*, as shown by the similar grouping of the three Graces in that painting. Botticelli was always fascinated by triadic ryhthms, and another example can be found in a group of angels in his late work, the

London *Nativity*. The angels in this drawing may have originated, as types, in such Verrocchio models as the terracotta angels for the Forteguerri monument, but Botticelli has drawn his with a subtlety of highlighting which is worthy of Leonardo. One recalls other indications that these two artists experienced a strong community of artistic life, even perhaps worked and conversed in the same studio: the passage in the *Treatise on Painting* which mentions "Our Botticella," and the other in the *Codice Atlantico* which begins "Sandro!"

The *St. John the Baptist* in the Uffizi (Plate 2) is another of Botticelli's rare drawings in which superior quality makes the authorship unquestionable. As a type, the Saint also recurs in the *Trinity* belonging to Lord Lee of Fareham, at Richmond, and in the later (1488) *St. Barnabas altarpiece*, but, as Berenson has suggested, the work most immediately akin to this drawing is the fresco of *St. Jerome* in the Church of Ognissanti, executed in 1480 in rivalry with one by Ghirlandaio. Botticelli's fresco belongs to the period preceding his journey to Rome, and it shows an appreciable growth of emphasis upon feeling, resulting in a harsher, more broken style which is definitely reminiscent of Andrea del Castagno.

The most complex of Botticelli's drawings, *Abundance* or *Autumn* (Plate 9), in the British Museum, belongs either to the Roman period or to the years immediately following, and not to the period of the *Primavera*, as is often erroneously stated. The obvious similarity between this figure and that of the woman carrying the bundle of wood in *The Leper's Sacrifice* in the Sistine Chapel, makes the dating of the drawing certain. The enormous cornucopia, the elongation of the left arm and of the moving foot, the rotundity of the putti, all strongly correspond to the distinguishing characteristics of this period in which Botticelli's style reached its peak of plastic expansiveness. One can clearly see what techniques he used thanks to the differing stages of completion of the various parts of the drawing: he sketched first in black crayon, went over this in pen, then added watercolor and white lead highlights. The paper is delicately tinged with pink, a color which he almost always chose in the preparation of his paper and which plays an important part in accentuating the subtleties of his chiaroscuro passages and of the highlighting.

The experience which Botticelli gained in his work on the Sistine Chapel frescoes was to dominate almost a decade of his life, reaching its culmination in the sculptural perfection of *The Birth of Venus* in the Uffizi and the *Mars and Venus* in London. I know of no drawings from this period, and the closest one in time, the *Angel* (Plate 4) in the Uffizi, already shows the stylistic transformation which occurred toward the end of that decade, when the artist passed from concern with plastic perfection back to his old interest in strongly accentuated linear sequences. As compared to his youthful works, however, there was now a new element of agitation and convulsion in his line. This drawing (Plate 4) used to be generally associated with the Ambrosiana *Tondo*, but it is on a far more advanced level stylistically, and clearly should be dated within the same years as the *Coronation* from San Marco, that is, around 1490. One can still see the old Verrocchio archetype in the drawing, but it is weightier even though the rhythm of the composition is more broken. The severe damage which this sheet has suffered makes all the more welcome the knowledge of an unpublished drawing in a private collection, an *Angel in flight* (Plate 5), which is from the same period and is in good condition.

The British Museum drawing of *Faith* (Plate 7) corresponds in style to the celebrated *Calumny of Apelles* in the Uffizi, of which the date is uncertain but is generally set at 1494–95. What seems new in the drawing is its pyramidal composition with a pronounced verticality to which Botticelli's familiar angular, convulsive line tends to adjust itself. Though the execution is free and brilliant, however, it is not as attractive as that of the youthful period because the compositional thematic element seems too forced; this can also be said of the Uffizi *Pallas* (Plate 6). In these drawings some remote traces of Verrocchio persist, but in the three fragments of an *Adoration of the Magi*, now divided between Cambridge and New York (Plates 11, 12 and 13), there are clear reminiscences, beautifully assimilated, of Leonardo's marvelous but unfinished treatment of the same subject. (The Botticelli drawing was a chiaroscuro preparatory study for a painting similar to the one in the Uffizi which he never finished and which was clumsily retouched in the eighteenth century.) Other drawings are so bound up with the style, varied as it is, of the *Divine Comedy* illustrations that there is no point in continuing any further without discussing the latter.

We are not really sure precisely when Lorenzo di Pier Francesco de' Medici commissioned Botticelli to illustrate *The Divine Comedy*, an enterprise which was to constitute the highest homage ever paid to Dante in the figurative arts; but the task, of long duration, certainly must have been accomplished within the 1490's. The greater part of the manuscript used to belong to the Berlin Kupferstichkabinett and I do not even know whether or not it has survived the destruction of the last war, in which so many works in the Kaiser Friedrich Museum were lost.* The remaining, and smaller, portion of the manuscript, which includes illustrations for seven cantos of the *Inferno* plus a general introductory drawing, is owned by the Vatican Library.

As can be seen from the three finished illustrations, of which we here include one detail (Plate 20), the drawings, prepared in silverpoint and gone over in pen, were originally meant to be carefully painted in watercolor, probably with the collaboration of assistants; the project, however, was abandoned, probably because it failed to satisfy Botticelli's concrete artistic demands. The fact that the original idea never reached completion explains some of the disconcerting aspects of this extraordinary series of illustrations: first of all the total lack of chiaroscuro—the reduction of visual experience to simple contour lines. The minute detail with which the various episodes are depicted, in order to adhere literally to Dante's narrative, together with the lack of any synthesis or perspective in the Renaissance sense, creates a strange effect to which it is sometimes difficult to become accustomed. Obviously perspective is not altogether lacking, but it has been reduced to a sort of aerial viewpoint wherein the figures are crushed together and the effect often becomes simply that of a tapestry. In other words, these qualities are to a certain degree anti-Renaissance and altogether medieval, and are accentuated by the original conception of the illustrations as miniatures.

There is also a positive aspect to these "defects" in that they concentrated Botticelli's imagination upon pure line, which in his hands was never medieval or Gothic but unmistakably Renaissance in quality. In the *Inferno* drawings this is often accompanied by outspoken reminiscences of Andrea del Castagno and Pollaiuolo: for example, the centaurs shooting arrows (Plate 18), the damned souls in the very state of undergoing their flame-like transformation into serpents (Plate 21) or the gloomy nude figures of the sufferers from dropsy (Plate 22). For the viewer who can disregard certain prosaic passages, which may be called structural and most of which depict the tediously repetitive figures of the two poets, the individual groups in this series of drawings constitute a fantastic repertory of the richness which purely linear representation is capable of conveying. The *Purgatorio* and *Paradiso* illustrations represent a more evolved stylistic conception than do those for the *Inferno*; among the most extraordinary is the drawing of the prideful (Plate 23), who are organically fused to the blocks they carry while an admirably heroic portrayal of *The Justice of Trajan* forms the background. Another is Plate 24, in which the groups of penitents are drawn in full, curvilinear cadences. Still another depicts an enchanted, fantasmagorical vision of the terrestrial Paradise, in which the plants are drawn with a subtlety reminiscent of Leonardo.

But this almost inexhaustible richness of detail should not obscure the fact that in certain instances Botticelli also managed to achieve the perfect synthesis of a given scene. For example, in his illustration for Canto I of the *Paradiso* (Plate 26), the visual impact is rigorously

* PUBLISHER'S NOTE: Sheets 8 and 17 through 34 of the *Inferno* and 1 through 8 of the *Purgatory* are still extant in the Kupferstichkabinett of the Berlin-Dahlem Staatliche Museen. The remainder of the *Purgatory* sheets and those for the *Paradise* are in East Berlin.

unified by his reiteration of the circular motif and by his balancing of the figure group centrally within an ethereal space whose depth would be impossible to measure geometrically. As for the little trees, it has been justly observed that they bring to mind the delicacy of Oriental work, but it is also true that they are suffused with a profoundly Christian, human tenderness. Another illustration which manages to be strongly unified in its own way is the one for Canto XIII of the *Inferno* (Plate 19). Even though its composition is not centralized, there is powerful synthesis of another kind in the bold two-dimensional reduction of the forest, seen from above and presented as a tapestry.

In discussing these drawings, Botticelli's line deserves special consideration; it does not always maintain the same degree of expressive power. It is worthwhile to compare those rare passages which remain as simple silverpoint with the majority, which have been gone over in pen; for example, note the illustration for Canto XXI of the *Paradiso* (Plate 28). The figure on the ladder is miraculous in its power of suggestion, as opposed to the two standing figures. Even Botticelli could not always manage to preserve the freshness of a drawing once he began to go over it.

There are, as I mentioned earlier, other surviving Botticelli drawings which have a direct relationship to the *Divine Comedy* illustrations. Among the best of all the master's drawings is the subtle, fleeing figure (Plate 16) in the Uffizi, which resembles figures in certain of the groups of damned souls (as in the illustration for Canto XXIX of the *Inferno*, Plate 22). Then there is the beautiful, flame-like *Pallas* in the Ambrosiana (Plate 17), which is not unlike certain angels in the *Purgatorio* illustrations (such as that for Canto XV, Plate 24).

We know of no dated works in any medium from the final period of Botticelli's life except the famous London *Nativity* of 1500, with its inscription alluding to one of Savonarola's apocalyptic predictions. The drawing of the same subject in the Uffizi (Plate 30) has been associated with this painting because it has the same configuration of the Virgin and Child, but from the point of view of its linear style it seems to have been executed earlier. In any case it is hard to give any meaningful appraisal of it because although it is an evocative drawing, it has been so often retouched with watercolor.

On the other hand, a work which does clearly correspond stylistically to the London *Nativity* in the wave-like overlapping of its lines is the extraordinary monochrome painting imitating a gilded bronze relief and forming part of *The Story of Virginia*, in the Accademia Carrara in Bergamo (Plate 31). While this is not a drawing in the strict sense of the word, it might as well be; it employs the same means of pictorial expressiveness, and was conceived with the same immediacy. In any case it should be considered among Botticelli's most significant works. A group of rough boys, armed with clubs, is pursuing a group of little girls who are running for safety to the older women. There is a strong flavor here of the genre scenes of children's life often seen in northern European paintings, but Botticelli's composition achieves far greater compression and tension in its currents of agitation.

Finally, as a companion piece to the four paintings (divided now among London, Dresden and New York) illustrating *The Miracles of Saint Zenobius*, which are probably the latest of the artist's surviving works, we include the Darmstadt Kupferstichkabinett drawing, *The infidels and the Descent of the Holy Spirit* (Plate 32). Nothing could better attest to Botticelli's inexhaustible vitality.

BIOGRAPHICAL NOTE

ALESSANDRO di Mariano Filipepi, called Botticelli, was born in Florence in 1445 and died there in 1510.

Sandro was a pupil of Filippo Lippi, whose art made a lasting impression upon him. In 1470 and in 1472 he had his own atelier in Florence, into which, in turn, Filippino Lippi came as a pupil. The latter's father had died in Orvieto in 1469, having left Prato two years earlier. Documented works by Botticelli which have survived from this period are the *Fortitude* (1470) for the Sala del Magistrato della Mercanzia, now in the Uffizi, and the *St. Sebastian* (1474) for the church of Santa Maria Maggiore, now in the Staatliche Museen in Berlin-Dahlem. These and Botticelli's other works from this period demonstrate the originality with which he assimilated Verrocchio's and Pollaiuolo's ideas of form; he also felt the influence of the young Leonardo, with whom he was friendly. The influence of Leonardo was only partial, and in a single area, but it was certainly enlivening and is something which has not always been adequately taken into account. In 1475 Botticelli painted a standard for the Medici joust, and in 1478, after the quelling of the Pazzi conspiracy, he painted effigies of the hanged men on the façade of the Bargello. He was always strongly bound to the Medici and absorbed the atmosphere of Humanist culture which surrounded them; he was most particularly attached to Lorenzo di Pier Francesco de' Medici, for whom several of his most famous works were executed, including, eventually, the Dante illustrations. In these early years, inspired by Politian, Botticelli painted the *Primavera* which is his most famous youthful work. In 1481, together with Cosimo Rosselli. Piero di Cosimo, Ghirlandaio and Perugino, he was summoned to Rome by Sixtus IV to decorate the Sistine Chapel, and there he executed the three frescoes which still exist, depicting episodes in the life of Moses. In 1482 he returned to Florence and never left his native city again. Botticelli's activity was so extensive that it is impossible here even to mention all his major works. In the years following his return from Rome he painted the celebrated *Birth of Venus*, now in the Uffizi, the lost frescoes of the Villa dello Spedaletto, near Volterra, those for the Villa Lemmi, which are now in the Louvre, the *St. Barnabas altarpiece* and the *Madonna of the Magnificat*, both now in the Uffizi, and other works.

About 1490 (as in *The Coronation of the Virgin*, originally in San Marco but now in the Uffizi) a greater emphasis upon religious feeling began to manifest itself clearly in Botticelli's work; an intimate expression of this torment is the above-mentioned series of illustrations for *The Divine Comedy*. The intensity and profundity of this religiosity, however, does not point to Botticelli's having joined the Savonarola sect. It is also purely a figment of Vasari's imagination that he suffered extreme poverty in his old age. One cannot even say that there was any premature decline in his fortunes, for in 1502 Isabella d'Este's agent recommended him highly as a possible artist to decorate her Studiolo, which was not yet completed, and in 1504 he was one of the artists consulted by the Opera del Duomo to decide on a location for Michelangelo's *David*. However, in those years Florentine art had other goals: a taste for the colossal and an increasingly monumental and less interiorized approach, so that even in his late masterpieces, the *Episodes from the life of Saint Zenobius* (divided among London, Dresden and New York), Botticelli must have seemed almost anachronistic to his contemporaries by the time he died.

BIBLIOGRAPHICAL NOTE

There is a vast bibliography on Botticelli. The following list includes only the works which have been consulted in the preparation of this volume.

BERENSON, B.
The Drawings of the Florentine Painters, Chicago, 1938.

BETTINI, S.
Botticelli, Bergamo, 1942.

COLVIN, S.
Drawings of the Old Masters in the University Galleries and in the Library of Christ Church, Oxford, Oxford, 1903–1907.

GAMBA, C.
Botticelli, Milan, 1936.

I Disegni della R. *Galleria degli Uffizi in Firenze*, Florence, 1912–21 (Serie Prima, Portafoglio 3, text by P. N. Ferri).

LIPPMANN, F.
Zeichnungen von Sandro Botticelli zu Dante's Göttlicher Comödie, Berlin, 1887.

MESNIL, J.
Botticelli, Paris, 1938.

POPHAM, A. E., AND P. POUNCEY
Italian Drawings . . . in the British Museum, London, 1950.

RAGGHIANTI, C. L.
Notes and essays. "Un 'Corpus Photographicum' di Disegni" in *La Critica d'Arte*, XVI–XVIII, August–December, 1938, p. xxvi.

VASARI, G.
Le Vite . . ., Milanesi edition, Vol. III, Florence, 1906.

VENTURI, A.
Il Botticelli interprete di Dante, Florence, 1921.

VENTURI, A.
Botticelli, Rome, 1925.

VENTURI, L.
Botticelli (Phaidon Press edition), Paris, 1949.

YASHIRO, Y.
Sandro Botticelli, London-Boston, 1929.

I would like to express deep thanks to my friends David Carritt and Francesco Arcangeli, who brought the unpublished drawing (Plate 5) to my attention.

LIST OF PLATES

I

Head of an angel. Silverpoint with white lead highlights on prepared paper. 20 × 17 cm.

RENNES, MUSEUM, #494.

2

Saint John the Baptist. Pen, watercolor and white lead on rose-colored prepared paper. 36 × 15.5 cm.

FLORENCE, UFFIZI, #188.

3

School of Botticelli: *Profile of a young woman.* Silverpoint heightened with white lead on yellow-pink prepared paper.

OXFORD, ASHMOLEAN MUSEUM.

4

Angel. Pen, watercolor and white lead highlights. 27 × 18 cm.

FLORENCE, UFFIZI, #202.

5

Angel in flight. Pen, watercolor and white lead highlights. 9.2 × 9.5 cm.

BOLOGNA, PRIVATE COLLECTION.

6

Pallas. Black crayon and pen with white lead highlights on rose-colored prepared paper. 22 × 14 cm.

FLORENCE, UFFIZI, #201.

Sandro botticello

7

Faith. Pen, over a sketch in black crayon; white highlights. 25 × 16.6 cm.

LONDON, BRITISH MUSEUM, MALCOLM, #12.

8

School of Botticelli: *Pallas*. Pen, watercolor and white lead on rose-colored prepared paper.

OXFORD, ASHMOLEAN MUSEUM.

9

Abundance. Black crayon, pen, watercolor, white lead highlights, on rose-colored prepared paper. 31.7 × 25.3 cm.

LONDON, BRITISH MUSEUM, MALCOLM, #11.

10

St. Thomas receiving the Virgin's girdle. Pen and white lead highlights over a crayon sketch on tinted paper. 17.5 × 12 cm.

MILAN, BIBLIOTECA AMBROSIANA, CODEX RESTA, F. 19.

11

Adoration of the Magi. Fragment, central portion. Chiaroscuro in tempera on canvas. 30 × 23 cm.

CAMBRIDGE, FITZWILLIAM MUSEUM.

12

Adoration of the Magi. Fragment, right side. Chiaroscuro in tempera on canvas. 44 × 37 cm.

CAMBRIDGE, FITZWILLIAM MUSEUM.

13

Adoration of the Magi. Fragment, left side. Chiaroscuro in tempera on canvas. 17.5 × 19.5 cm.

NEW YORK, MORGAN LIBRARY.

14

School of Botticelli: *Death of Saint Marina*. Pen and watercolor. 26 × 10.5 cm.

TURIN, BIBLIOTECA REALE, INV. #15594.

SANTA MARINA

15

School of Botticelli: *Resurrection of a youth.* Pen and watercolor with white lead highlights on rose-colored paper. 16 × 14.5 cm.

FLORENCE, UFFIZI, #1149.

16

Fleeing figure. Pen and watercolor. 13.5 × 16 cm.

FLORENCE, UFFIZI, #160 F.

17

Pallas. Pen. 19 × 6.6 cm.

MILAN, BIBLIOTECA AMBROSIANA, CODEX RESTA, F. 14.

18

The Divine Comedy: Inferno XII. Detail. Pen over silverpoint preparation on parchment.

ROME, VATICAN LIBRARY.

19

The Divine Comedy: Inferno XIII. Detail.

ROME, VATICAN LIBRARY.

20

The Divine Comedy: Inferno XVIII. Detail. Pen over silverpoint preparation, entirely painted in various watercolors, on parchment.

BERLIN-DAHLEM, KUPFERSTICHKABINETT.

21

The Divine Comedy: Inferno XXIV. Detail.

BERLIN-DAHLEM, KUPFERSTICHKABINETT.

22

The Divine Comedy: Inferno XXIX. Detail.

BERLIN-DAHLEM, KUPFERSTICHKABINETT.

23

The Divine Comedy: Purgatorio X. Detail.

EAST BERLIN, KUPFERSTICHKABINETT.

24

The Divine Comedy: Purgatorio XV. Detail.

EAST BERLIN, KUPFERSTICHKABINETT.

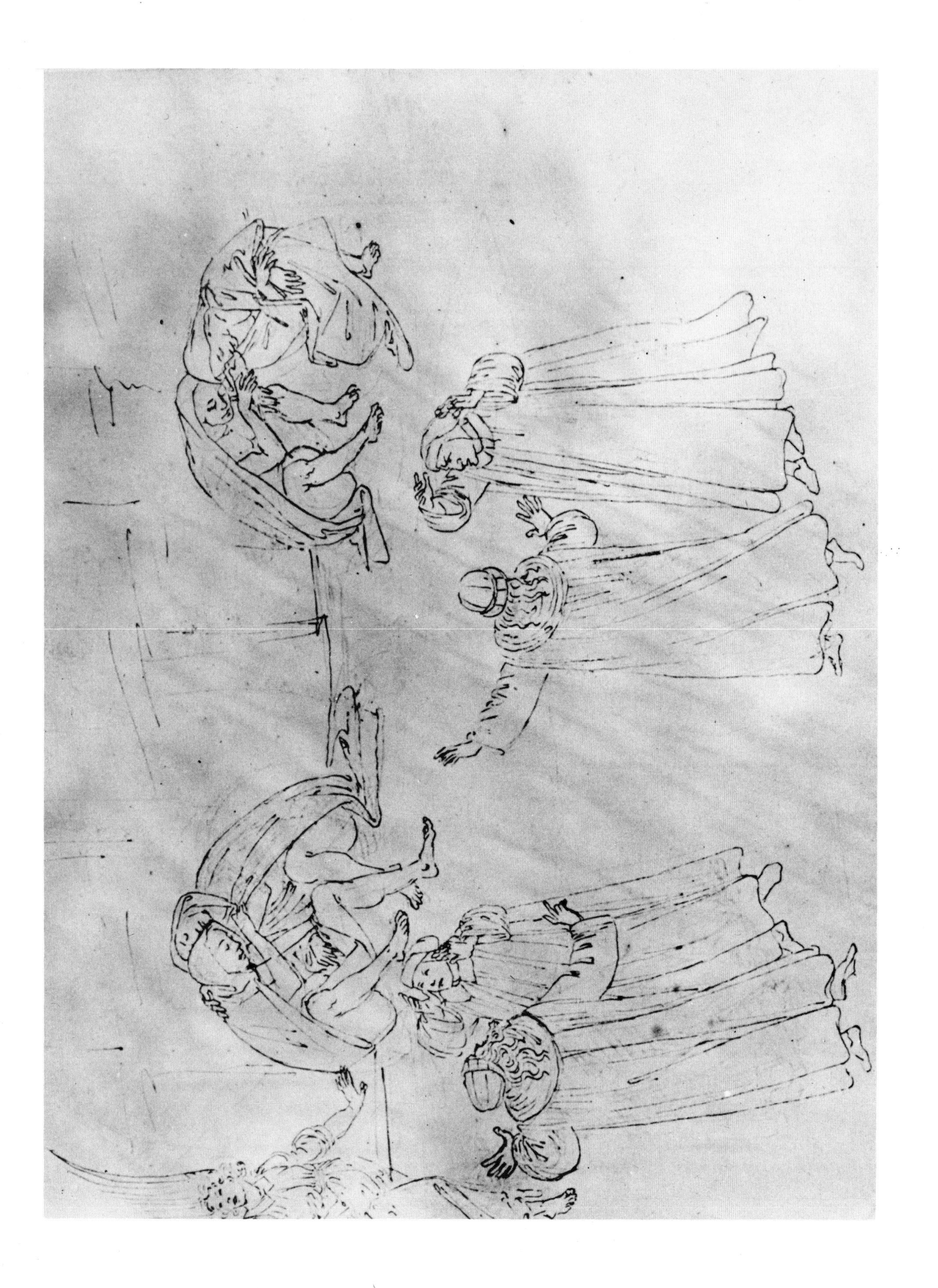

25

The Divine Comedy: Purgatorio XXXIII. Detail.

EAST BERLIN, KUPFERSTICHKABINETT.

33

26

The Divine Comedy: Paradiso I. 32 × 47 cm.

EAST BERLIN, KUPFERSTICHKABINETT.

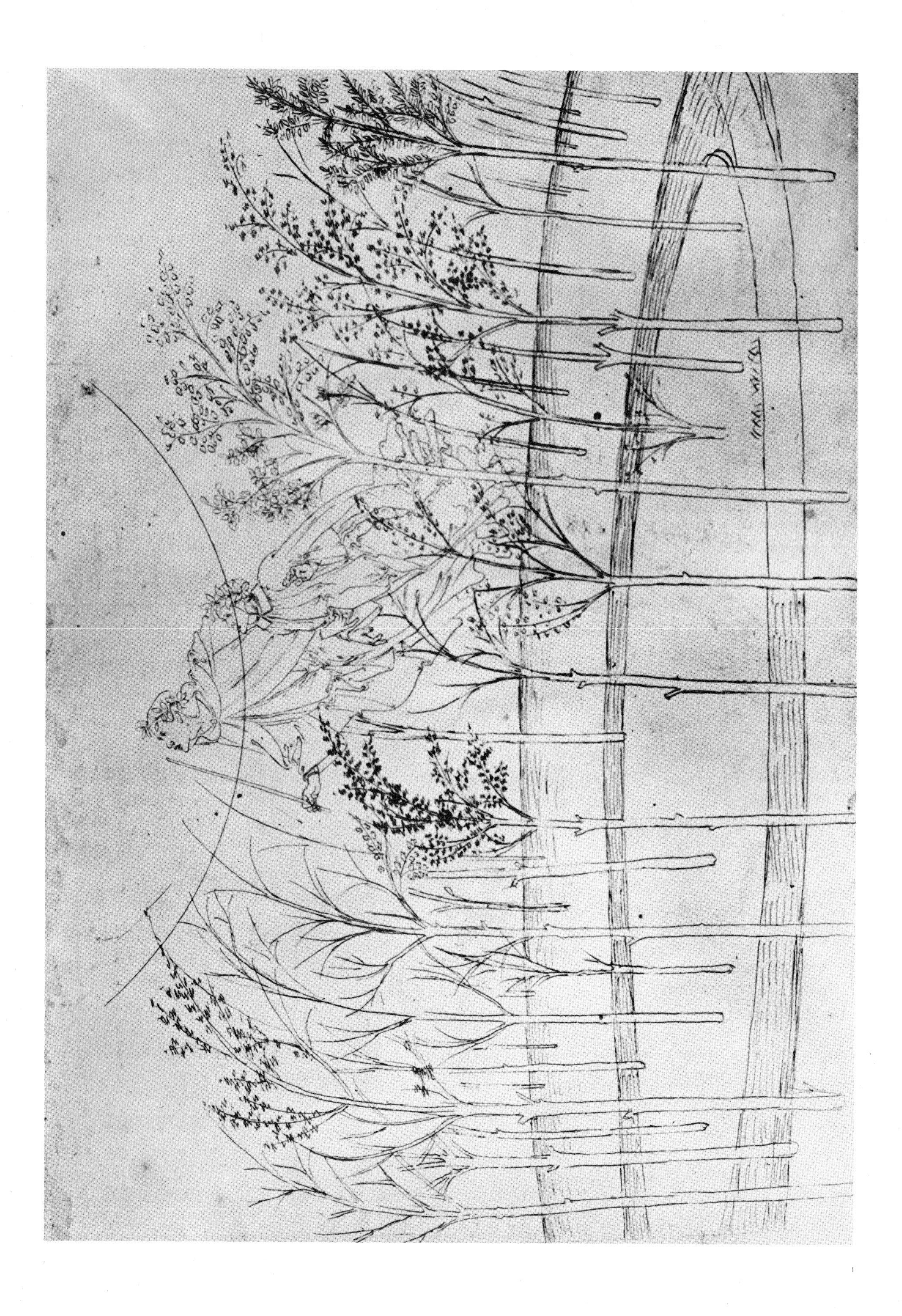

27

The Divine Comedy: Paradiso XX.

EAST BERLIN, KUPFERSTICHKABINETT.

quando cholui 20

28

The Divine Comedy: Paradiso XXI.

EAST BERLIN, KUPFERSTICHKABINETT.

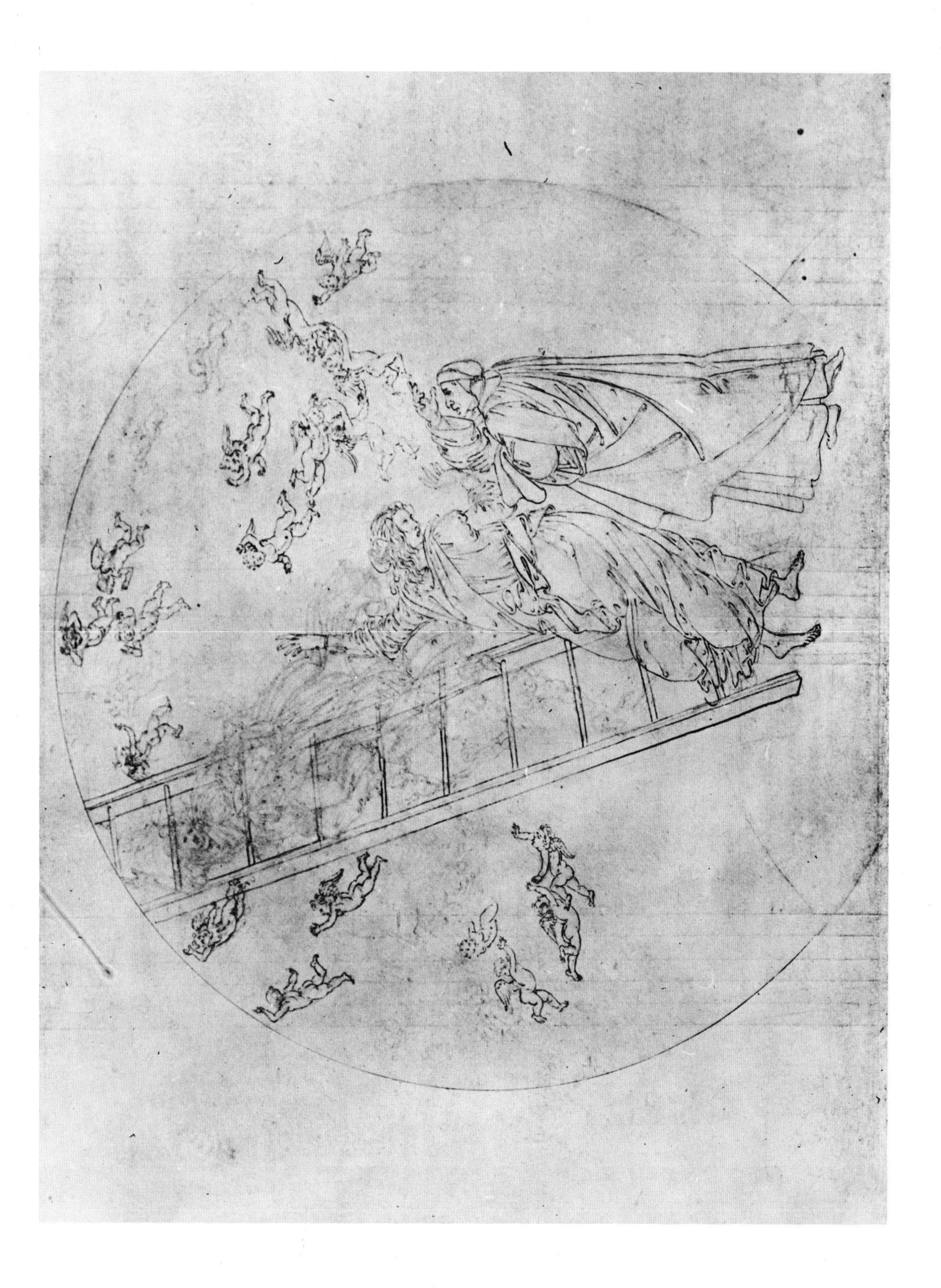

29

The Divine Comedy: Paradiso XXIX. Detail.

EAST BERLIN, KUPFERSTICHKABINETT.

30

The Nativity. Pen and watercolor with white lead highlights, on rose-colored prepared paper. 16 × 26 cm.

FLORENCE, UFFIZI, #209.

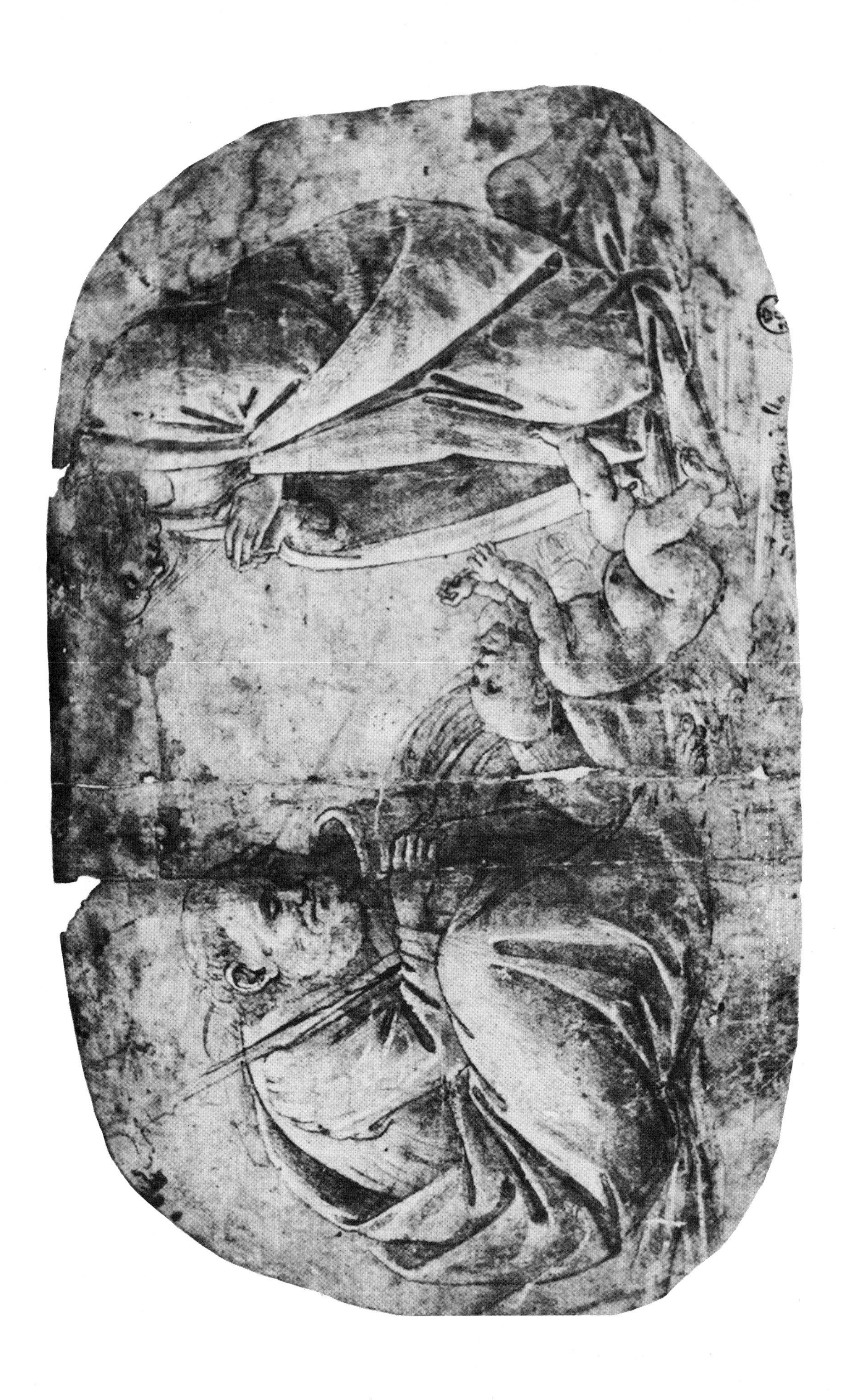

31

Monochrome detail of "The Story of Virginia." Tempera on wood panel.

BERGAMO, ACCADEMIA CARRARA.

32

The infidels and the Descent of the Holy Spirit. Pen, watercolor and white lead highlights.

DARMSTADT, KUPFERSTICHKABINETT.